THE POPCORN BOOK

Tomie de Paola

THE
POPCORN
BOOK

Holiday House · New York

FOR FLORENCE NESCI,
*who taught me how
to pop the best popcorn
in the whole wide world*

Library of Congress Cataloging in Publication Data

De Paola, Thomas Anthony.
  The popcorn book.

  SUMMARY: Presents a variety of facts about popcorn
and includes two recipes.
  1. Popcorn—Juvenile literature. [1. Popcorn]
I. Title.
TX799.D46   641.6'5'677   77-21456
ISBN 0-8234-0314-9
ISBN 0-8234-0533-8 (pbk.)

HERE IT IS....
"Popcorn is best stored in a tight jar in the refrigerator, so the kernels keep their moisture."
BOY, THIS IS INTERESTING! LISTEN....
P
P

"Popcorn is the oldest of the three main types of corn. There is field corn, which we feed to animals like cattle and pigs; sweet corn, which is the kind we eat; and popcorn."

"Popcorn was discovered by the Indian people
in the Americas many thousands of years ago.

"One of the first sights Columbus saw
in the New World was the Indians in San Salvador
selling popcorn and wearing it as jewelry."

"But popcorn is even older than that.
In a bat cave in New Mexico, archeologists found
some popped corn that was 5,600 years old."

"The Indian people of the Americas
had many different ways to pop popcorn.
   "One way was to put an ear of corn on a stick
and hold it over a fire.

   "But many kernels were lost in the fire
with this method."

"Another way was to throw the kernels right into the fire by the handful.

"The popcorn popped out all over the place, so there was a lot of bending and running around to gather it up."

"In 1612, French explorers saw some
Iroquois people popping corn in clay pots.

"They would fill the pots with hot sand,
throw in some popcorn, and stir it with a stick.
"When the corn popped, it came to the top
of the sand and was easy to get."

"The Iroquois people were fond of popcorn soup."

"The Algonkians who came to the first Thanksgiving dinner even brought some popcorn in a deerskin pouch.

"The colonists liked it so much that they served popped corn for breakfast with cream poured on it."

NOW, HERE'S THE PART I READ FIRST.

"Popcorn is best stored in a tight jar
in the refrigerator, so the kernels
keep their moisture.

"If the kernels dry out, there will be
too many 'old maids' left at the bottom of the pan.
'Old maids' are unpopped kernels."

IT DOESN'T LOOK
LIKE ENOUGH.

"If the popcorn does dry out,
you can add one or two tablespoons of water
to the jar and shake it
until the water is absorbed."

"Popcorn pops because the heart of the kernel
is moist and pulpy and surrounded
by a hard starch shell.
  "When the kernel is heated,
the moisture turns to steam
and the heart gets bigger until
the shell bursts with a 'pop.'"

"The Indian people had a legend that inside
each kernel of popcorn lived a little demon.
When his house was heated,
he got so mad that he blew up."

"There are different kinds of popcorn: White hull-less and yellow hull-less are the ones most commonly sold in stores.

"The smallest type is called 'strawberry' because it has red kernels and the ears look like strawberries.

" 'Rainbow' has red, white, yellow, and blue kernels. It is sometimes called 'Calico.'

"There is black popcorn, too, but all of it pops white.

"The biggest kernels are called 'Dynamite' and 'Snow Puff.' "

SHAKE-
SHAKE-
SHAKE-

"After popcorn is popped, most people like to put melted butter and salt on it.

"But if salt is put in the pan before the kernels are popped, it makes the popcorn tough."

"There are many stories about popcorn.
One of the funniest and best-known
comes from America's Midwest.

One summer, it was so hot and dry
that all the popcorn in the fields
began to pop.

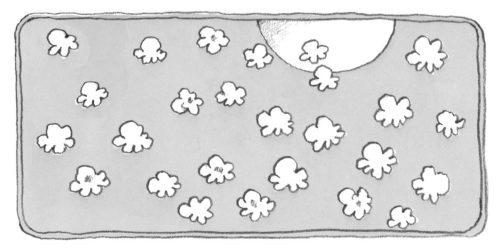

In no time at all, the sky was filled
with flying popcorn.

It looked so much like a blizzard,
everyone put on mittens and scarves
and got out the snow shovels."

TWO TERRIFIC WAYS TO POP CORN*

EVERYDAY WAY

1. Heat a heavy, 3-quart saucepan (with a cover) over high heat for about 2 minutes.
2. Pour about ¼ cup of cooking oil into the pan. It should cover the bottom.
3. Lower heat to medium high.
4. Add 3 or 4 kernels.
5. When they pop, add just enough popcorn to cover the bottom of the pan. (Don't add more than ½ cup.)
6. Lower heat, cover pan, and shake.
7. When popping stops, pour into a bowl. Add melted butter and salt.
8. Eat!

be sure to ask a grown-up first

FRIDAY NIGHT POPCORN
Florence Nesci's recipe

1. Put some vegetable shortening (like Crisco) into a large skillet that has a cover.
2. Melt the shortening over low heat.
3. Add enough popcorn to barely cover the bottom of the pan. The shortening should cover the popcorn. Add more if necessary.
4. Stir constantly until 1 or 2 kernels pop. (The kernels will swell and be very tender.)
5. Put on cover and raise heat and shake very fast until all the corn is popped.
6. Pour into a bowl and salt it. No butter is necessary.
7. Eat and enjoy it!

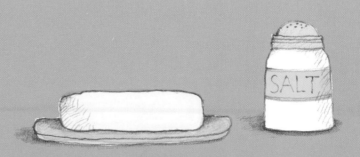

SALT